HOW DO FROGS SWALLOW WITH THEIR EYES?

Questions and Answers About Amphibians

BY MELVIN AND GILDA BERGER
ILLUSTRATED BY KAREN CARR

SCHOLASTIC REFERENCE

CONTENTS

KEY TO ABBREVIATIONS

cm = centimeter/centimetre
kg = kilogram
km = kilometer/kilometre
m = meter/metre

Text copyright © 2002 by Melvin and Gilda Berger
Illustrations copyright © 2002 by Karen Carr
All rights reserved. Published by Scholastic Inc.
SCHOLASTIC, SCHOLASTIC REFERENCE, and associated logos are trademarks and/or registered trademarks of Scholastic Inc.

No part of this publication may be reproduced, or stored in a retrieval system, or transmitted in any form or by any means, electronic, mechanical, photocopying, recording, or otherwise, without written permission of the publisher. For information regarding permission, write to Scholastic Inc., Attention: Permissions Department, 557 Broadway, New York, NY 10012.

Library of Congress Cataloging-in-Publication Data

Berger, Melvin
    How do frogs swallow with their eyes? : questions and answers about amphibians /by Melvin and Gilda Berger ; illustrated by Karen Carr.
        p. cm. -- (Scholastic question and answer series)
    Summary: Presents information about frogs, toads, newts, salamanders, and caecilians in a question-and-answer format.
    1. Amphibians--Miscellanea--Juvenile literature. [1. Amphibians--Miscellanea. 2. Questions and answers.] I. Berger, Gilda. II. Carr, Karen, 1960- ill. III. Title.
QL644.2 .B473 2003   597.8--dc21   2001042641

ISBN 0 439 26677 7

Book design by David Saylor and Nancy Sabato

10 9 8 7 6 5 4 3 2   03 04 05 06 07

Printed in the U.S.A.   08
First trade printing, March 2003

Expert reader: Mark Halvorsen
Senior Wild Animal Keeper
Central Park Wildlife Center
New York, NY

The amphibian on the cover is an Azure poison arrow frog.
A Van Dyke's salamander appears on the title page and an Eastern newt is on page 3.

To Cindy Guntharp and the boys and
girls of the Hamilton School
— M. AND G. BERGER
To my grandmother, Louise Maxwell, my
Computer Fairy, and my uncle, Gary Maxwell,
my Computer Gnome
— K. CARR

INTRODUCTION

You may have the wrong idea from fairy tales that frogs are ugly, annoying creatures. Or, you may mistakenly believe that you get warts from touching toads. Perhaps you even think that frogs and toads can help witches and wizards perform magic.

Well, it's time to discover the truth about frogs and toads, salamanders and newts, and caecilians—the animals we call amphibians.

For example, did you know that amphibians:

- live a "double life" on land *and* in water?
- can breathe through their skin?
- almost never drink water or any other liquid?
- swallow their food alive and whole?
- range in length from under $1/2$ inch (1 cm) to over 5 feet (1.6 m)?

Amphibians may not be warm and fuzzy. But their striking ways make them some of nature's most fascinating creatures!

Melvin Berger   Gilda Berger

WHAT AMPHIBIANS ARE

How do frogs swallow with their eyes?

Easily. When swallowing a big mouthful of food, a frog blinks its eyes. The blinking pushes the frog's huge eyeballs down on top of its mouth. This helps squeeze the food in its mouth into its throat. WHOOSH!—down goes its meal!

What kind of animals are frogs?

Amphibians. These are animals that can live in water and on land. The word comes from the Greek word *amphibios,* which means "double life."

Most frogs and other amphibians hatch from eggs in water. Many later move onto land. But even land amphibians usually live near water. Almost all go into the water to breed and lay their eggs.

How many kinds of amphibians are there?

Almost 5,000 different species, or kinds. Frogs and toads make up the largest group with about 4,000 species. Salamanders and newts are a much smaller group—just over 400 different kinds. The smallest group of all is the caecilians (see-SIL-ee-ans) with fewer than 200 species.

What do salamanders and newts look like?

Like lizards. But lizards are reptiles, not amphibians. Lizards have scales on their skin and claws on their toes. Salamanders and newts don't.

Leopard frogs

Common frog

Common toad

Do caecilians look like salamanders?

No. Caecilians look like worms. Soft-bodied and without legs, caecilians burrow in the soil. But caecilians are amphibians, not worms. The biggest grow to be more than 2 feet (60 cm) long!

Caecilians have sharklike heads and curved, sharp teeth for hunting worms, insects, and other creatures that live underground.

Are frogs different from toads?

Not really. Frogs and toads belong to the same group of amphibians, named Anura. The word means "tail-less." Scientists often use the term "frogs" to refer to both frogs and toads.

In most cases, however, you can see differences between frogs and toads. The European frog, for example, is like many other frogs. It has smooth and moist skin, with a small, thin body; long legs; and big, bulging eyes. The European toad, on the other hand, is like many other toads. It has dry, lumpy or warty skin, a stout body, short legs, and smaller eyes.

Almost all frogs live in or near water. Many toads make their homes in drier places.

Do amphibians have hair or feathers?

No. Amphibians have a smooth, slippery skin covered with a slimy fluid called mucus (MYOO-kuhss). The mucus is like the secretion inside your nose, mouth, and throat. In amphibians, mucus comes from glands in their skin.

Amphibians are vertebrates (VUR-tuh-britz). That is, they have a spine or backbone. They are also cold-blooded animals, just like fish and reptiles. That means their bodies keep to about the same temperature as the air or water around them. Like fish and reptiles, most amphibians lay eggs.

Which is the biggest amphibian?

The Japanese salamander. It can grow to be 5 feet, 4 inches (1.6 m) long and weigh 88 pounds (40 kg). That's about the same size and weight as a 13-year-old!

The smallest amphibian is the Cuban tree toad. At a length of less than ½ inch (1 cm), it can easily fit on your thumbnail!

Amphibians range in size from very small to quite large. But it may surprise you to learn that most of them are less than 2 inches (5 cm) long!

Japanese giant salamander

Which is the biggest frog?

The Goliath frog. One caught in Africa in 1989 measured 34½ inches (89 cm) from snout to toes with legs extended. Stretch out your arms to the sides as far as they will go. A Goliath frog could almost reach from fingertip to fingertip!

African Goliath frog

How do amphibians breathe?

In various ways. Young amphibians and some adults breathe through gills, like fish. The gills take in oxygen from the water in which these amphibians live.

As the amphibians grow, many lose their gills. They develop lungs for breathing air and are able to go onto land. Some adults have both lungs and gills.

All amphibians also breathe through their thin, moist skin. Their skin can take in oxygen on land or in water. Amphibians obtain from 25 to 80 percent of the oxygen they need to stay alive through their skin. In most cases, the larger the skin area, the more oxygen passes through.

Do amphibians drink water?

Rarely. Amphibians get most of the water they need through their skin, not by mouth. Water passes through their skin like oxygen does.

Certain toads, such as the red-spotted toad, have a strange way of taking in more water. These amphibians sit down in damp or wet places. The water they need comes in through their baggy bottoms!

Do amphibians shed their skins?

Yes. Frogs split their skins and slide them up toward their mouths. Sometimes frogs swallow their old skins! Caecilians, newts, and salamanders unroll their skins from head to tail like a snake does. Some water species, though, just let the old skin float away.

How often do amphibians shed?

It varies. Green tree frogs may get rid of their old skin every day. The African clawed toad sheds its skin every five to seven days. But many toads shed every 10 days.

Green tree frog

Molting frogs usually eat their skin.

What do amphibians eat?

Almost any living creature that they can catch and fit into their mouths. Frogs and toads dine mainly on insects and small animals. Very large frogs, like the bullfrog and ornate horned frog, also eat mice, small rats, baby birds, lizards, young turtles, and snakes. Some fill their bellies with smaller amphibians or eat their own eggs or those of other species. Water amphibians usually capture fish, pond worms, snails, and small crabs.

Worms and insects make up most of the diet of salamanders and newts. Caecilians usually seek out slow-moving animals with soft bodies, such as worms.

Tiger salamander

Boat-backed ground beetle

How do amphibians find food?

Some sit and wait for prey to pass by. Tiger salamanders, for example, hide until a crawling insect or worm comes into sight. Then, the salamander opens its mouth and flicks out its long, sticky tongue. With one quick swoop, the salamander nabs and swallows the prey.

Caecilians creep up on earthworms and other soft, slow crawlers. Then the amphibians make a quick grab, gripping their prey with their small, sharp teeth.

Do any amphibians hunt for food?

Yes. Many frogs and toads leap around looking for prey. When a European common frog sees a beetle, for example, it bounds forward. The frog shoots out its tongue, nabs the insect, and pulls the bug into its mouth. One blink of the frog's eyes, and the prey is gone.

Toads are slower feeders than frogs. They generally stalk their prey, like cats. Sooner or later, the toad moves within range of its dinner. A quick tongue-flick and—well, you know the rest!

Caecilian

Earthworm

Is an amphibian's tongue like yours?

No. Frogs, toads, and a few kinds of salamanders have long, strong, sticky tongues with M-shaped tips. The tongues are attached near the front of the mouth, not in the back like yours. This lets these amphibians catch and flip food into their open mouths faster than your eyes can see.

Do amphibians chew their food?

No. Amphibians usually swallow their food alive and whole. Their tiny teeth are used to grasp the prey and position the food in the right way for swallowing.

Do frogs and toads have good eyesight?

Yes. Good eyesight helps frogs and toads find food and avoid being eaten. Their gigantic, bulging eyes let them see in almost every direction. Frogs and toads are especially able to see anything that's moving.

Also, frogs and toads are usually farsighted. They can easily spot prey or enemies that are 40 to 50 feet (12 to 15 m) away. But place a live cricket under their noses and they have trouble seeing it.

Do amphibians have good senses of smell and taste?

Yes. Amphibians have two sets of organs for smelling—in the mouth and at the tip of the snout. The sense of smell is especially important for amphibians that live in the water.

Scientists know less about amphibians' sense of taste. Most amphibians will eat anything. But some frogs and toads are very fussy. If one swallows a bad-tasting ant or wasp, the amphibian throws up its entire stomach. The organ hangs out of its mouth until the bad food drops out. Then the amphibian swallows its stomach—and looks for something good to eat.

Common bullfrog

Do amphibians have ears?

Frogs and toads do—but they don't look like your ears. All you can see are two flat, round disks behind and below their eyes. These are the eardrums. Other parts of the ears are hidden inside their heads.

Hearing is one of the most valuable senses of frogs and toads. They use it to find mates and to avoid coming too close to other amphibians.

Salamanders and newts do not have ears. But they can pick up vibrations from the ground with their front legs and lower jaws. Experts believe that caecilians use their bodies to feel vibrations in the ground.

Do amphibians make sounds?

Yes. Most frogs and toads croak, squeak, or grunt by forcing air from their lungs over their vocal cords. The air blows up their throats like balloons. In some frogs, the throat becomes as big as the rest of the animal!

Salamanders, newts, and caecilians are almost all silent. At most, they make a few kinds of clicking or popping sounds. Some may squeak or hiss when in danger.

Pine Barrens tree frogs

How do amphibians cool off in very hot weather?

Simply. On very hot days, the amphibian moves to a shady spot or jumps into the water. If the weather turns cold, the amphibian goes to a place where it can bask in the sun's warmth.

Amphibians in warm regions do not usually hibernate. These animals stay active all year-round. Some may estivate (ESS-ti-vate). They sleep away the extreme heat of summer in damp holes, called burrows.

How do amphibians keep from freezing in winter?

Some hibernate (HYE-bur-nate). Amphibians in cold areas pass the winter in a deep sleep, called hibernation. Some rest in burrows they dig under the earth. Others settle into the mud at the bottom of a lake or pond. Here they stay until the warm weather returns.

Northern leopard frogs

HOW AMPHIBIANS GROW

When do frogs and toads find mates?

Mostly in the spring or start of the rainy season. That's when it's warm and wet enough for breeding, or having young.

For most of the year, frogs and toads live alone. But in order to breed they must find partners and mate. The male frogs and toads start to sing to the females. The females are attracted by the mating calls.

What do frog and toad calls sound like?

Trills, bellows, chirps, hiccups, bleats—there are so many different sounds! The call of each frog and toad species is different and wonderful.

Often many male frogs or toads sound off at the same time. As more and more join in, the male chorus grows very loud. In the spring you may hear a chorus of trilling American toads or bellowing bullfrogs calling to the females.

Do female frogs and toads call back?

No. Most females are silent at mating time. But at other times of the year they make sounds like the males of their species. Usually they're not as loud.

How do male caecilians court females?

No one knows. Caecilians are rare, shy animals that spend most of their time underground. That makes them very hard to watch or study.

How do salamanders and newts find mates?

Mostly by smell. Salamanders and newts lack vocal cords. Instead, the males give off a particular odor that attracts the females. They either rub against the females or wave their tails to send out the odor.

Longtailed newts

How many eggs do female amphibians lay?

From one to several thousand. Among frogs and toads, fertilization, or the joining of egg and sperm, takes place outside the female's body—usually in the water. Among salamanders and caecilians, fertilization occurs inside the female—before she lays the eggs.

Cuban tree toads and some poison arrow frogs lay only a single egg. Common frogs and common toads produce from 1,000 to 3,000 eggs. Salamanders, newts, and caecilians usually lay a few dozen eggs at a time.

Where do female amphibians lay their eggs?

Usually in the water. Most frogs lay their eggs in a mass, called a spawn, on the surface or bottom of a pond. Toads usually lay their eggs in long chains wrapped around rocks or the stems of water plants. Newts and salamanders also attach round masses of eggs to plants growing in the water.

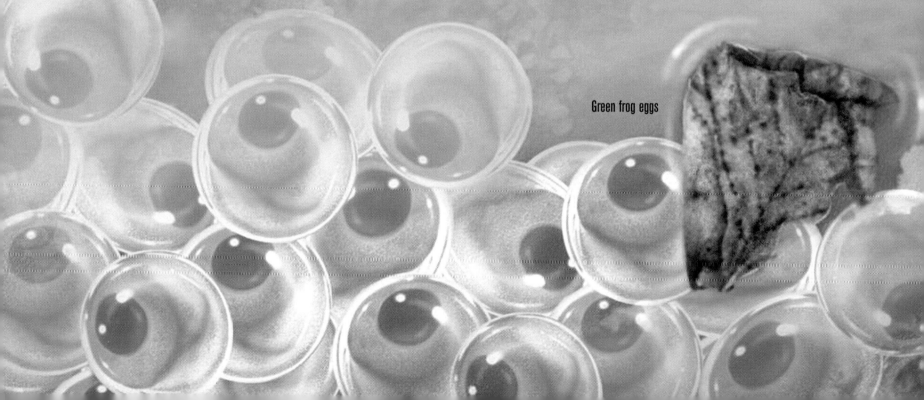

Green frog eggs

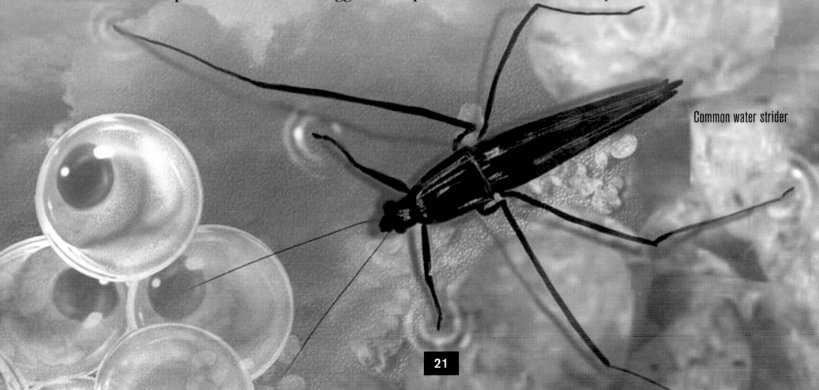

Do any amphibians lay eggs on land?

Yes. Some tiny bromeliad (bro-ME-lee-ad) frogs lay their eggs high in the trees of the rain forest. They place the eggs in tiny pools of water that form within the leaves and petals of certain plants called bromeliads.

Others, such as the red-eyed tree frog, place the eggs in a leaf that hangs over water. As the eggs hatch, the baby frogs fall into the water.

Certain land-dwelling salamanders and caecilians lay clusters of eggs in moist soil near springs, ponds, or streams.

Which amphibians do not lay eggs?

A few species of toads, some salamanders, and about half of all caecilians. These amphibians give birth to live young. African live-bearing toads and Alpine salamanders are two species in which the eggs develop inside the mother's body.

Common water strider

Do amphibian females care for the eggs?

Most don't. The females lay the eggs and leave. Only some stay around to protect the eggs from predators, which are animals that hunt for their food. Caecilians usually wrap their bodies around their eggs to guard them.

Do any frogs swallow their own eggs?

Yes. Female brooding frogs and some others swallow their eggs. But they don't really digest them! The eggs stay in the mother's stomach until they grow into little frogs, called froglets. When the young frogs are ready to leave their mothers, the females open their mouths and the froglets swim out.

Which female amphibian carries her eggs until they hatch?

The marsupial frog of South America. This frog has a back pouch where she puts the fertilized eggs. When the young have grown into froglets, the mother pulls open her pouch. The little froglets paddle away.

After mating, the skin of the female Surinam toad of South America swells up. It forms a thick, spongy layer on her back. The male presses the 50 or so eggs she has laid into this layer. The eggs stay here until they hatch, about three months later.

Are male amphibians good parents?

Some are. The male midwife toad of Europe wraps the female's string of 35 to 50 eggs around his hind legs. All day he hobbles around with the eggs attached. At night the male heads to a pond or stream to soak the eggs in the water. After about four weeks, he drops the eggs into water, where they hatch.

The South American male Darwin's frog does even more. He puts the eggs into his mouth and lets them slide into the baggy skin under his chin. When the eggs have grown into froglets, he lets them out.

Marsupial frog

Do all amphibian eggs hatch?

No. The little eggs have no shells or other protection. Fish, snakes, birds, insects, worms, and many other animals eat them. A sudden freeze, heavy rains, or a dry spell also kill some eggs. Experts tell us that only about 5 percent of all amphibian eggs ever hatch.

What is a newly hatched egg called?

A larva. The plural is larvae (LAR-vee). Each larva looks like a tiny fish, with gills for breathing, a flat tail, and tiny limbs or no limbs at all.

Frog or toad larvae are known as tadpoles or polliwogs. Newly hatched salamanders, newts, or caecilians are just called larvae.

NORTHERN RED-LEGGED FROG METAMORPHOSIS

Eggs

Tadpoles

How do tadpoles become adult frogs?

Through metamorphosis (met-uh-MOR-fuh-siss). The larvae slowly lose their gills and develop lungs. Back legs and then front legs grow. The body gets longer as the tail gets shorter, and finally the tail disappears.

The larvae are now adults. Some kinds of amphibians climb out of the pond and start life on land. Others spend the rest of their lives in the water.

How long does metamorphosis take?

Different times for different species. A spadefoot toad holds the record for the shortest period. It passes through metamorphosis in just 12 days. The bullfrog, on the other hand, needs three years to change from tadpole to adult. Some salamanders that live in colder waters can take up to five years to become adults.

Adult

Do caecilian, salamander, and newt larvae go through metamorphosis?

Yes. But salamander and newt larvae change less than frog and toad tadpoles. The larvae of caecilians hardly change at all. They already look like small eels or snakes.

How long do amphibians live?

No one knows for sure. In general, the bigger the amphibian, the longer it lives.

Experts tell us that frogs reach an age of about six to eight years. Salamanders live longer—up to 30 years. In captivity, one European common toad reached the ripe old age of 40. A Japanese giant salamander at the Amsterdam Zoo lived to be 52!

Caecilian metamorphosis

Ringed salamander metamorphosis

How do scientists tell a frog's age?

One way is to examine its bones. Just like trees, frogs' bones show a ring for every year.
By counting the rings, experts can tell how old a frog was.

Red spotted newt metamorphosis

WHERE AMPHIBIANS LIVE

Which amphibians are most widespread?

Frogs and toads. These amphibians live almost everywhere. Yet each seldom strays far from home. Most spend their entire lives within about 100 feet (30.5 m) of the place where they were born.

You find frogs and toads on every continent except Antarctica. Members of some species—common frogs, moor frogs, and wood frogs—even live within the Arctic Circle!

Why don't frogs and toads live in Antarctica?

It's too cold and icy. They cannot survive such freezing temperatures. Since frogs and toads are cold-blooded, they have no way to make heat inside their bodies. When a frog gets cold, it moves around less. When it's really cold, it hardly moves at all.

Where do salamanders, newts, and caecilians live?

Where the climate is moderate to hot. Salamanders and newts live in the temperate areas of the Northern Hemisphere—North America, Europe, and parts of Asia and Africa.

You find caccilians in hot, tropical zones. Here it is warm day and night—and all year-round.

Do amphibians live in the ocean?

No. Amphibians almost always live in or near freshwater in ponds and lakes, streams and rivers, swamps and marshes. Those that spend all or most of their time in water are called aquatic amphibians.

Cave salamander

Green salamander

Sierra Nevada ensatina salamander

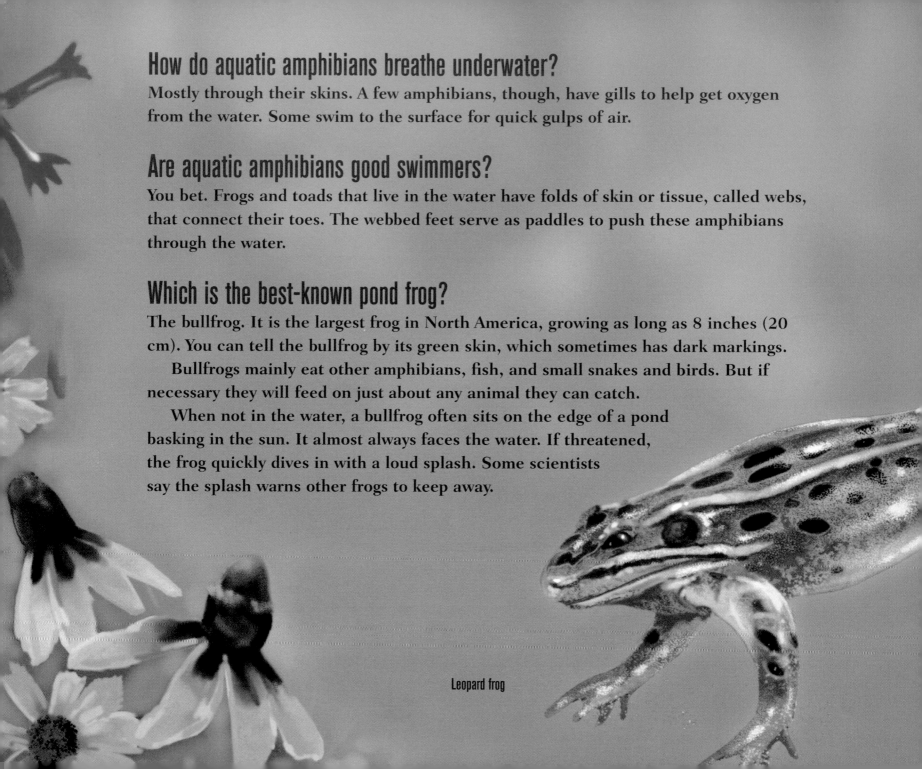

How do aquatic amphibians breathe underwater?

Mostly through their skins. A few amphibians, though, have gills to help get oxygen from the water. Some swim to the surface for quick gulps of air.

Are aquatic amphibians good swimmers?

You bet. Frogs and toads that live in the water have folds of skin or tissue, called webs, that connect their toes. The webbed feet serve as paddles to push these amphibians through the water.

Which is the best-known pond frog?

The bullfrog. It is the largest frog in North America, growing as long as 8 inches (20 cm). You can tell the bullfrog by its green skin, which sometimes has dark markings.

Bullfrogs mainly eat other amphibians, fish, and small snakes and birds. But if necessary they will feed on just about any animal they can catch.

When not in the water, a bullfrog often sits on the edge of a pond basking in the sun. It almost always faces the water. If threatened, the frog quickly dives in with a loud splash. Some scientists say the splash warns other frogs to keep away.

Leopard frog

Which amphibian moves from pond to woods to pond?

The red-spotted newt. This North American amphibian begins life in a pond. After hatching, the larva climbs out of the water and heads for damp woods. At this stage it is bright reddish-orange. The partly grown amphibian is called a red eft.

After about two or three years, the red eft changes color and becomes olive green. Now full-grown, it returns to the pond where it was born.

Which frogs live in streams and rivers?

Those that are best fit for living in running, not still, water. Such stream frogs as the tailed frog and the canyon tree frog have grasping fingers and toes. They cling to water weeds and rocks so they don't get swept away, even in swift flowing water.

Do any salamanders live in flowing water?

Some do. The largest of all salamanders, the Japanese giant salamander, and the smaller mud puppy salamander of the United States and Canada make their homes in rivers and streams.

Aquatic caecilians also live in running water. They hide in tunnels that they dig at the bottoms of streams and rivers.

Are wetlands good for amphibians?

Yes, very. Swamps, marshes, and bogs are covered with a shallow layer of water all or part of the year. Many tadpoles and larvae start their life here.

Plants that grow in the wetlands feed the larvae and provide hiding places for the adults. More insects and other animals that amphibians eat live here than almost anywhere else.

Pig frog

Texas toad

Ringed salamander

Which wetland amphibians are named for the sounds they make?

Spring peepers and carpenter frogs. Spring peepers announce spring in many parts of the eastern United States and Canada. Small tan or olive-green spring peepers form giant choruses, loudly singing "peep, peep, peep." You can sometimes hear them from 1 mile (1.6 km) away!

Carpenter frogs are brown with four yellow stripes down their backs. They live in coastal swamps of the eastern United States. Their call, "ca-took, ca-took, ca-took," sounds like two carpenters hammering nails—but at different times.

Leopard frog

Least bittern

Chicken turtle

Where do 80 percent of all frogs and toads live?

In tropical rain forests. Rain forest frogs are active most of the time. Small frogs, like the many different kinds of poison arrow frogs, also called poison dart frogs, continually hop around looking for something to eat.

Many kinds of frogs live high in the rain forest trees. These small, light frogs easily clamber over the twigs and leaves. Sticky pads on their fingers and toes help them climb and hold on to the branches.

What color are rain forest frogs?

All colors of the rainbow—from hot yellow, to strawberry red, to deep blue, to rich purple. Now guess the color of the tomato frog and the banana tree frog!

Can flying frogs fly?

No. But they do glide through the air from tree to tree. These frogs, such as the Wallace flying frog, have webs on their hands and feet that act like parachutes. The frogs can sail through the air as far as 50 feet (15 m)—the width of a basketball court!

Variable poison arrow frog

Tri-colored poison arrow frog

Red eyed tree frogs

Variable poison arrow frog

Azure poison arrow frogs

Lehmann's poison dart frog

Do amphibians live in grasslands?

Yes and no. Many frogs and toads live in land covered with grasses. But no salamanders, newts, or caecilians can be found there.

One of the best-known grassland frogs is the northern leopard frog of the United States and Canada. This green or brown frog takes its name from the rows of round or oval dark "leopard" spots on its back. A most striking feature is its gold-colored eyes with black horizontal pupils.

The leopard frog lives in meadows or fields far from water. When in danger, this frog quickly hops, zigzag style, toward the nearest pond.

Do salamanders live on land?

Yes. Many make their homes in rotting logs, rock piles, tangled roots, or burrows under the ground. Some, such as lungless salamanders, spend all their time in damp places. Since they lack lungs, the salamanders breathe only through their skin, which must stay moist to absorb oxygen.

Land caecilians usually crawl through moist soil or under leaf litter or rotting logs.

Do any amphibians live in hot, dry deserts?

Yes, a few do. During the day, desert-dwelling frogs and toads often hide in cool burrows they dig in loose sand. Some toads, called spadefoot toads, use hard, sharp growths on their back feet like tiny shovels to help them dig.

Inside the burrow, a desert frog or toad may eat an occasional worm or bug that passes by. But when the sun sets, the frogs and toads come out to look for crickets, beetles, and other small creatures. During a rare rain shower, they hop out to mate and lay eggs in mud puddles.

Tarantula

New Mexico spade footed frog

HOW AMPHIBIANS PROTECT THEMSELVES

Which animals prey on amphibians?

The list is very long. That's because amphibians live both in and out of water.

Amphibians that live on land have to protect themselves from snakes, birds, lizards, and mammals, including rats, weasels, skunks, and foxes. In the water, amphibians must look out for fish, otters, water snakes, and many kinds of wading birds.

What is an amphibian's best defense?

Camouflage. Amphibians' skin colors and markings help them blend in with their surroundings. A predator, such as a snake, finds it hard to spot the brown Asian horned toad. It looks like bark, twigs, or dead leaves on the forest floor.

Camouflage also helps an amphibian catch its meal. A small bug or other animal may think the green tree frog is a leaf—until it's too late.

One thing is very important about camouflage. The amphibian must not move— or all is lost!

Why do some amphibians have bright colors?

To warn away predators. Brightly colored frogs and toads usually have very powerful poisons on their skin. The colors are like traffic lights. They warn of danger.

Most of these poisons are bad-tasting. They irritate the mouths of predators and can even kill them. Many predators learn a lesson after biting bad-tasting, colorful frogs. From then on, the predators avoid frogs with those colors.

Smith frog

Geographical tree frog

Oriental fire-bellied toads

Do amphibians use color to scare predators?

Yes. Some amphibians suddenly show a bright color to surprise or shock a predator. The small Oriental fire-bellied toad, for example, usually sits quietly among the weeds in a pond. Its green-and-black back makes it very hard to see. If a predator comes too close, the toad arches its back, kicks open its legs, and show its bright red, orange, or yellow belly. The attacker freezes in shock—and the fire-bellied toad hops away.

Does bluffing protect amphibians?

Yes. Looking big and fierce when you're small can be good protection. Upon meeting a snake, the Eurasian common toad puffs itself up. It also stands as tall as possible and tilts forward as though it's about to charge. Only a brave snake will not flee such a frightening sight!

Which amphibians use poison for defense?

Most do. Amphibians are covered with a poison that comes from glands in the skin. Some also have big, bulging poison glands. If an enemy presses or bites one of these, the poison squirts out. It gets a shot of burning, painful poison in the face!

Can touching a toad cause warts?

No. But touching the skin of some toads can burn your hands. If you rub your eyes afterward, your eyes may sting. Putting your hand in your mouth may make your tongue go numb—just like getting novocaine at the dentist.

Which amphibians have enough poison to kill you?

The tiny poison arrow frogs of Central and South America. A drop of poison from one of these frogs could kill 1,000 people!

Is slippery skin a good defense?

Yes, indeed. Many predators find it difficult to hold on to amphibians because they are so slippery. The prey slide right out of their grasp. Slippery skin comes from the mucus glands in the skin. If you've ever tried to hold a frog, you know what we mean.

Do amphibians ever run away from predators?

Yes. Amphibians hop, jump, swim, slither, or run away from predators. One frog, the African clawed toad, can actually jump backward!

Some amphibians dive into a pond or stream to escape. Others hide beneath logs or rocks, or find other safe places. A few kinds dig their way backward into sand or soft mud, leaving only the fronts of their snouts and their eyes showing.

Do amphibians fight back?

Yes. Some frogs and toads kick to break the grip of a predator holding them. These amphibians often aim their blows at the enemy's head.

The limbs of salamanders and newts are much too small to be used for kicking. But frantic squirming and wiggling often breaks a predator's grasp.

Do frogs bite?

Most do not. But the horned frog of South America is an exception. If a predator approaches, the horned frog hops forward and snaps its mouth shut. More than one scientist trying to study these frogs has been bitten on the hand. The biting frog buries its teeth in the person—and holds on like a bulldog.

Hognose snake

Green frog

Southern long-toed salamander

Which amphibians hide for protection?

Several kinds of salamanders. The salamanders known as waterdogs and mud puppies, for example, live in the water and spend their days under rocks or debris. Only at night do they venture out to look for prey.

Do salamanders bite?

Some do. The fiercest is the amphiuma, the largest salamander in North America. The amphiuma can give a nasty, painful bite if you're not careful. Other species of biting salamanders include mountain dusky, black-bellied, and seal salamanders.

Salamanders bite more fiercely than frogs because salamanders have more teeth. While many frogs and toads have teeth only in the upper jaw, salamanders usually have upper and lower teeth. Some even have teeth on the roof of the mouth!

Do salamanders use their tails for protection?

Yes. A salamander sometimes raises its tail and wags it from side to side. This may lead a predator to attack the tail instead of the head. Since most of the salamander's poison is on its tail, the attacker gets a mouthful of poison.

A predator may bite or pull the tail off! The salamander is no worse for the loss. But the shocked predator usually drops the tail. The tail jumps and wiggles on the ground for up to 15 minutes. That's time enough for the salamander to escape, leaving its twitching tail behind.

Can salamanders grow new tails?

Yes. Both salamanders and newts can grow new tails. It may take as long as two years for a slightly shorter new tail to grow in. During that time, however, the salamander moves more slowly and is less able to fight off attackers.

Who are amphibians' worst enemies?

People. Pollution, cutting down rain forests, and filling in ponds and wetlands destroys the places where amphibians live. Poisons in the environment can either harm or kill amphibians. Among the most dangerous are the chemicals used to kill pests and the acid rain that forms from car exhaust and factory smoke. These can either harm or kill amphibians.

Also, humans eat millions of tons (tonnes) of frogs every year. In many poor countries frogs are a major source of protein. In some developed countries frog legs are considered a treat.

Are some amphibian species dropping in numbers?

Yes. In recent years at least two species of amphibians—gastric brooding frogs of Australia and golden toads of Central America—are believed to have become extinct. No one has seen one of these for years. Also, about 30 different species of amphibians are on threatened or endangered animal lists. Among them are the largest amphibian, the Japanese giant salamander, and the largest frog, the Goliath frog.

How can you protect amphibians?

In many ways. Learn all you can about amphibians. Write to government officials and ask for laws to save and protect frogs and other amphibians. Join a community or school group that is working to clean up ponds where amphibians live. Urge friends to help save the amphibians.

If you have the space, you can make a garden pond. The pond should have shallow and deep areas and be as large as possible. Be sure the water is at least 2 feet (60 cm) deep so it doesn't freeze solid in the winter. Place plants and logs around the sides to provide hiding places for adult amphibians. Enjoy your amphibian visitors!

Red eared slider

Pickerel frogs

Spring peeper

Three-lined salamander

INDEX

About the Authors

The Bergers welcome every spring with trips to nearby ponds to spot peepers and listen to their calls. "Hiking in the woods to find the returning frogs and salamanders is great fun," they say.

About the Illustrator

When she was a child, Karen Carr's greatest treat was spending the summer at her grandmother's house. She says, "At night my sister and I collected toads from the flower beds, admired them, and let them go near the lake. Of course they were back in the flower beds the next night!"